SPIRIT, SHOW the WAY

CONFIRMATION PRAYERS based on THE FRUITS OF THE HOLY SPIRIT

Margaret Felice

TWENTY-THIRD PUBLICATIONS

twentythirdpublications.com

Twenty-Third Publications
One Montauk Avenue, Suite 200
New London, CT 06320
(860) 437-3012 or (800) 321-0411
www.twentythirdpublications.com

Cover illustrations: ©Shutterstock.com / mamanamsai
and ©Shutterstock.com / Macrovector

ISBN: 978-1-62785-545-7
Printed in the U.S.A.

 A division of Bayard, Inc.

Contents

INTRODUCTION

WHAT ARE THE "FRUITS OF THE SPIRIT"? These are qualities that are evident in people who respond to the grace of the Holy Spirit: love, joy, peace, patience, kindness, goodness, generosity, gentleness, faithfulness, modesty, self-control, and chastity. Many of these qualities are also found in a list that St. Paul included in his letter to the Galatians. Since the earliest days of Christianity people have recognized that good things grow in those who let God work in them. Jesus himself said in one of his parables "by their fruits you will know them."

This is a time in your life when you are hearing a lot about growth: growing pains, growth spurts, maybe even the occasional comment that you can't do something until you are grown. You will experience spiritual growth during this time of physical growth, but it's not something that stops once you reach your full height or final shoe size. Hopefully, you have been allowing these qualities to grow in you, with God's grace, for many years already. They will continue to grow for many years to come.

As a teen, you are making decisions right now about what kind of person you want to be, and you are building the habits that may shape your life forever. You don't do this alone. Friends, family, and role models all influence your growth, and through the sacrament of confirmation the Holy Spirit gives gifts that help you to be a virtuous person.

These prayers will help you focus your mind and heart on asking God for what you need. God is always ready to give us more than we ask for and to help us grow slowly and with strength, like a good tree bearing good fruit.

Love

WHAT IS THERE TO SAY ABOUT LOVE, other than everything? It's the biggest of big ideas, the thing that motivates most of our actions, what we spend our whole lives trying to find. There is a liturgical prayer that says, "Love is our origin, love is our constant calling, love is our fulfillment in heaven." It's what we come from and what we are made for. Wow.

If our human nature were perfect, love would always come naturally to us. Since human nature is flawed, though, we let other desires get in the way of living love. But even when we are farthest from the right path we never stop looking for love. We can be tempted to seek it in a lot of things that will never love us back: popularity, fame, drugs, alcohol, wealth, fashion, prizes, or accomplishments. Part of growing in love is being open to the awareness of God's love and of our worth as beloved children of God.

When we grow in love we act more for others than for ourselves. We never stop wanting what is best for others, even in the middle of conflict. We put people before any temptations in the world.

Romantic love is a sliver of this larger life of love (even though early days of excitement can make it seem like the whole world). With time, healthy romantic love settles into a mutual trust and reliance. You learn more about what it means to want the best for someone, and about the freedom you find in knowing you are loved without condition.

Hopefully you have people in your life who give you a taste of what God's unconditional, everlasting love is like. And hopefully you, with the help of the Holy Spirit, will grow into someone with a heart big enough to share such a big love with others.

Prayer for remembering God's love

Spirit of love, you love me!
This can be hard to remember,
    harder still to understand.
The Bible says God is love, and that Jesus
    was sent to earth out of love.
You created me because you love.
Even when things don't go my way, or when I am
    feeling confused or alone, I am loved.
This means I have worth and value.

This means I should show love to my body,
mind, and soul.
This means I was made to share love.
Your fruits are signs of your love. May I always
be grateful and aware.

Close your eyes and breathe deeply. With each breath,
imagine God's love moving deep into your heart.
Do this for at least ten breaths.

Prayer for parents

Spirit of family, my parents are among the most
important people in my life right now, and they
likely will be forever. No matter what they've
done, no matter how I came to them, they are part
of me. This is one of life's great mysteries.

Give me eyes to see the ways that they love me,
especially when I feel annoyed or angry.

Give them whatever strength and consolation
they need, especially those things I'm too young to
understand or provide.

Help us all adjust as our relationships change,
and to have love at the center of our family life.

If you live with your parents, make an extra effort to be loving toward them today. If you don't, consider reaching out with a text or phone call, or simply thank the people who act as parents in your life.

Prayer of gratitude for the Church

Spirit who came at Pentecost, thank you for enlivening the Church for thousands of years. You have seen the Church through times of hardship and sadness. Now I can be part of this ancient community. I can receive the sacraments and grow closer to you, and I can gather with others to learn and to praise.

Remain with our Church so that we can serve and pray with energy and love. The Church is a community of love. Even though we fall short, I want to make loving choices and live up to Jesus' words from the Gospel of John: "This is how all will know that you are my disciples, if you have love for one another."

Educate yourself today on what life is like for Catholics in other parts of the world.

Prayer to keep friends safe

Spirit of care and concern, as a young person, I don't have much power, and neither do my friends. There may be times when someone close to me is a victim of someone with more power, someone who uses that power wrongly. I feel helpless just thinking about it.

Still, every time I let someone know they can share their pain with me, I help to make them safer.

Help me to listen well and be attentive to problems friends may have. Help me to be fearless in calling out abusive behavior, no matter the consequences. When I am overwhelmed or afraid, help me to know how to bring about healing.

Listen closely to your friends.

Joy

JOY IS A LOT LIKE HAPPINESS, ONLY BETTER! It is more than just a good feeling; it is a good feeling that comes from connection with God and with others—and that strengthens that connection as well. A conversation full of affection and laughter, the awareness that we are loved, the feeling of doing something you are meant to do—all of these lead to joy. The word "joy" appears often in the Bible, in hymns, and in prayers. The angels announce to the shepherds "good news of great joy": the news that Jesus was coming into the world. We are open to that joy every time we are open to God and to others.

Joy helps us to know what we are meant to do in our lives. God gives us interests and enthusiasm to help us know where our talents can be best used. Even when we have to do boring things that don't excite us, we can be motivated by joy because these tasks let us use our concentration or commitment or hard work.

Joy is meant to be shared. You can demonstrate for others what it is like to enjoy life, or you might lighten someone else's load so that they can focus on the joyful elements of life. Imagine what our world would be like if we could all be motivated by joy!

Prayer for having fun

Spirit of excitement, even though I am not a little
    kid anymore, I still love to play.
I can feel self-conscious about how much I want
    to have fun.
I want to shine bright with laughter and joy,
    but I fear standing out.
When I should worry less about what others think,
    can you ease my mind?
I am not ashamed of my longing for fun,
    and I count on you to show me how
    to ensure others are having fun too.

*Enjoy moments of fun, knowing they are a gift
from God.*

Prayer for enjoyment of studies

Spirit of all knowledge, I study so many things, and I see in my teachers what it is like to love a topic. Guide me to recognize the subjects that interest me and to go the extra mile when I'm curious to learn more.

I pray, too, that even if I am not excited about a subject I can be motivated by the challenge of learning and feel pride in knowing that I have grown by learning more.

What can you do to go the extra mile in your studies? Choose one thing you can do in a class that will help you learn, and do it.

Prayer for tryouts and auditions

Spirit of enthusiasm, you give me a passion for the sports and arts I pursue. This passion has driven me to grow in skill and interest, and now it is time to demonstrate that growth. Sharing that love with others can be frightening; now I have to share the thing that means the most to me and invite others to judge it. Never let me forget that I am a beloved creation of God with unique talents and interests, so that I can be confident and show everyone all that I have to give. Thank you for this gift of an activity that I love so much.

> *Think about all the smaller skills that go into being successful in your chosen activity. Thank God for helping you to grow in skills large and small.*

Prayer for discovering my vocation

Spirit of direction, when I feel joy and deep satisfaction, that is a sign that I am where I'm meant to be. Paying attention to joy in my heart can help me see what clubs to join, what classes to take, and what activities to stick with as I get older.

Whether there are big decisions to make or not, help me learn to be attentive to joy. Maybe you'll send me guidance in a lightning flash. More likely, you will help me see the direction of my life as I wake up every morning and try to make decisions that move me—and those around me—into greater joy, a joy that has your love at its core.

> *When you are doing something that really fires you up, savor that feeling of excitement.*

Peace

IN A WORLD FULL OF STIMULATION AND INFORMATION, PEACE MAY FEEL LIKE AN ABSENCE, or like the empty-ing of our brains and hearts. Yet peace, which Jesus offers so often in the gospel, is a presence, not an absence. It is a gift. It is knowing where you are and that God is beside you. It is knowing you can weather any storm that will come.

Peace is a feeling deep down that your worth comes from being a child of God and not from any accomplishments. This knowledge that our worth does not depend on what we do, that we do not have to earn God's love, can free us from preoccu-pations and refocus us on what matters.

Life presents many challenges to peace, and you may find yourself overwhelmed by anxiety or worry. God is not angry when we don't have peace, but God wants to pour peace into our hearts. Can you open yourself, even a little bit, to make space for God's peace? God may work through the clinical help we seek to deal with anxiety or depression too.

We model peace for others when we react to hardships with perspective and balance, confident that God will be there for us no matter what, and that God doesn't need our overreactions to be aware of what we need.

When there's a hardship or disruption in your life, you probably want to be done with it right away; you want things to go immediately back to the way they were. If you're able to deal with things not being exactly perfect all the time (or ever), you're growing in patience.

Prayer for times of sadness

Spirit of deep emotion, when I am hurt or discouraged or grieving, I wish there were a wall I could build around my heart to keep the sadness out. Since the breath of your peace moves through all things, good and bad, keep me from hardening my heart. I can grow in compassion when I experience hard times. I can grow in companionship when I ask for help. I can grow in courage when I face things as they truly are. Fill my broken heart with consolation and peace.

If you feel a wave of sadness, invite Jesus to sit beside you and experience it with you.

Prayer for school safety

Spirit of security, the tragedies I see on the news
make me anxious.

These stories make daily life feel dangerous,
reminding me how much of life is surprising
and out of my control.

You inspire peace in the world. You want safety
in the world. But the truth is that the world
doesn't always cooperate.

What can I ask you for? Protection?
Inspiration? Calm?

I ask for all these things because I know God
wants to be close to me in my worries, and
because even in an unpredictable world I have
faith in God's power and love.

I pray to be a sign of peace in my community.
I pray to know peace in the whole world.
And while I wait for the day of peace,
I pray for peace in my soul.

I pray for the safety of all children and people,
with all my heart.

*Offer a deep, slow prayer for the health
and safety of all students.*

Prayer for when I lose someone

Spirit of consolation, my heart is empty.
My whole world is changed. The way I imagined
my future, and who I thought would be in it,
has shattered.

Peace won't feel like forgetting.
Peace won't feel like nothing bad happened.
Peace won't feel like there's no hurt.

Because I know you love us all, I believe you can
help me keep finding good in the world, even
though I'm hurting. You can help me see that life
goes on, even in my pain.

Even if I can't envision it, there will be peace in
my heart someday, a peace that is strong enough
to exist alongside grief, a peace that fits like a
puzzle piece beside the love that makes grief deep,
the love that makes life holy.

Share your grief with God, even if you are angry.
Share your love for the person you miss.

Prayer for the first day of school

Spirit of new beginnings, I am full of feelings:
excitement, nervousness, and curiosity.
Calm me down when my emotions run over;
energize me if I'm not feeling ready.
Help me to be who I really am today, knowing
that's who I am meant to be, and that there's
no need to pretend to be someone I'm not.
Help me not be self-centered, and help me notice
others who might need encouragement
or friendship today.
Open my eyes to all the possibilities that await
me, and be beside me as I begin to explore.

*Before you enter the school building, take a deep
breath and smile.*

Patience

YOU WILL NEED PATIENCE AT SOME POINT IN YOUR LIFE. Enduring a yearlong course that's not your favorite, going months without knowing what your post-high school plans are, figuring out your career, deciding if and whom to marry—each of these (and countless more situations in life) will come with a long stretch of not knowing how things are going to end up.

When you think about it, we don't know how life is going to end up at all. Maybe rather than living lives of certainty with some stretches requiring patience, we should accept that we live mostly with uncertainty, with rare moments of sureness.

Like many virtues, patience can grow in us when we practice it, even when we're not feeling it. Next time you're in line, be alone with your thoughts rather than immediately seeking distraction on your phone. Slow yourself down, and you might stop craving the rush of stimulation, or you might just learn how to be okay with waiting.

Though you should try to let all of these fruits grow in you, from a practical perspective patience is one that you are really, really going to need. You can't do anything about the big questions in life. You can't do anything about all the things you'll have to wait for. Patience will help you get past the stress of waiting and enjoy each moment of the gift of life.

Prayer for siblings

Spirit of brotherhood and sisterhood, help me to love and care for my siblings. Help me to find more moments of fun than of frustration. Help me to react to them with calmness, treating them the way I want to be treated. I want to deepen the special bond we have to support one another and to learn to support others from the lessons I learn at home.

Hold back on saying a critical or unkind word to a sibling, even if you think it would get a laugh or make you look good.

Prayer to not grow up too fast

Spirit of every age, even though I feel "in between," your love helps me understand that I am exactly who I am supposed to be right now. It's a relief to feel complete just as I am, not more than I was, or less than I might be.

Comfort me when my youth feels like a deficiency, counsel me when I want to skip ahead to a time that I imagine will make me feel like more. In this moment I am enough.

The gifts I have to share at this age are needed. My questions, my energy, my enthusiasm: these are all precious to you, even if people around me treat them as an inconvenience. I pray I can resist underestimating who I am by rushing into what I might become.

How are you different now from how you were a year ago? What talents and interests do you have at this point in your life that you can explore?

Prayer for when I want control

Spirit of acceptance, my whole life
    others have made decisions for me.
I'm ready to be in charge of my own life!
But there are still choices that aren't mine
    to make, and sometimes I lash out
    when I don't get my way.
I am still waiting to be in charge of my life.
I need some calm in my heart to accept this
    waiting, a calm I'll probably need
    even when I'm older.
For now, though, I pray to learn to wait
    for the responsibilities and decisions
    that come with growing up,
and to be patient with those who are still
    making decisions for me.

*If you feel like someone is doing something for you
that you would rather do yourself, thank them instead
of acting annoyed.*

Prayer for slowing down

Spirit who waits for us, every day is filled with goals: get to school, do my work, finish practice, go to bed. It's tempting to always focus on what is next and to rush through my days.

Draw my attention to the world around me, to the realities I can touch and feel. Help me also perceive those things I can't touch or feel, such as your presence, the joy of my friendships, and the love of my family.

Being attentive is a type of prayer. I breathe deeply, and you fill me up. This breath awakens my senses and connects me to my surroundings. I am present. I am aware. I am listening. I am in no rush.

During those moments when you have to wait— in the lunch line, in class, for your ride to pick you up—value that moment of slowing down rather than trying to fill the quiet time with activity or distraction.

Kindness

PSALM 103 DESCRIBES GOD AS BEING "RICH IN," OR "FULL OF," or "abounding in" kindness. I love this image of kindness as something that fills us up and overflows into our relationships. If our sinfulness comes from emptiness, one way to avoid sin might be to ask the Spirit to fill us with kindness.

Kindness comes from within us. It is more than superficial "niceness"; it is motivated by the love that puts others' needs before our own. It doesn't ask for accolades, acknowledgment, or attention but finds its reward in living out the love we were made for.

When I was younger, I thought that in a life of limited resources, if I spent any of myself on kindness it would take away from the other things I was trying to do. Put another way, I wasn't as kind as I could have been. I have since learned that when we are kind, all of the resources grow because we can rely on each other and we support one another. Kindness doesn't diminish what we have; it increases what we have.

Kindness often shows itself in the simple tasks of our daily lives, but growing in kindness can anchor us when larger sacrifices are asked of us. It can help us accept others as they are and act in their best interest. Being good to others is a sure sign that the Spirit is working in our midst.

Prayer to be kind online

Spirit who encourages positive speech, are you busier now that the internet exists? So many people use it to be crude or cruel, or to show off how clever they are with a cutting remark. I am tempted daily to do such things.

When someone posts a picture, guide me to "like" instead of writing a critical comment.
When someone writes something I disagree with, guide me to listen, to ignore it if appropriate, or to disagree with respectful words if necessary.
When a peer is kind to me online, guide me to respond similarly rather than rejecting them.
All people have dignity, even if I only see them on a screen.
Guide me to build others up and to do my part to make the digital world a little kinder.

*If you use social media, post an uplifting
comment today.*

Prayer for helping a new student

Spirit of welcome, things get shaken up when a
new student arrives. All the routines we've grown
into now have a new person in them. This is not
an inconvenience but an opportunity.

It must be hard to be the only one adjusting to
this place that I already know well. If I give my
attention to a new person, maybe I can figure out
what will make them feel at home. Keep me from
being self-centered, so I don't make assumptions
or only help in the ways that I think are best. Open
my ears to listen and to learn from this stranger
who may soon be my friend.

*Reflect on your social interactions recently.
Were there any times when you excluded someone?
Think about how you can be more inclusive.*

Prayer for putting others before myself

Spirit who cares for all people, I'm often focused on my own needs: breakfast in the morning, time to finish homework, all the right gear for after-school activities. How much of the space in my head is focused on myself? I try to be good to others, but too often I only do those kind acts that fit into my life and my needs.

True kindness requires me to switch my focus. I want to be a person who shares true kindness, who doesn't do these things for show but because I'm thinking more of others than of myself.

You, Spirit, are always moving, seeking, and blessing. Help me to also search, so that I can find the needs of others and worry less about my own.

Who are the people in your daily routine whom you look past? Greet them today.

Prayer for when I don't know what to say

Spirit of silence and speech, my words don't
always obey my heart.

I see a friend in pain, and I want to reach out, but
am unsure what they need to hear.

Can you give me the words that will let them
know I am there for them and that I wish they
felt better?

Even if I don't find the words, I can be beside
them in silence, sharing my heart with my
presence more than my words.

*Send a quick text to a friend who is struggling to let
them know that you are thinking of them.*

Goodness

"BE PERFECT, JUST AS YOUR HEAVENLY FATHER IS PERFECT" (Mt 5:48). Yikes! That's a challenging command!

We are held to a high standard because we can meet that standard. Jesus believes in us and believes we can be truly good. The call to goodness is itself a reminder of how good we can be. Because God wants what is good for us, when we follow God's law we are growing in goodness.

Loving your neighbor? Goodness. Honoring your father and mother? Goodness. Forgiving? Goodness. Being humble and merciful? Goodness.

Being called to goodness could be intimidating if not for two things: God's endless capacity to forgive us when we stumble, and the companionship of the Spirit, nudging us toward the right path and speaking to us through our conscience.

Every little decision can be guided by goodness. A moment's thought about meeting God's standards is all it takes, and before you know it choosing goodness will be second nature.

Prayer to be light for the world

Spirit of brilliance, how am I meant to shine?
The world needs my light, but I can't force it to
  shine on my own. It starts with you.
When you give me light I can be patient, helpful,
loving, and kind. I can brighten my environment
by thinking of others more than myself.

I want to bring that light into all that I do, so that
the gifts you give and fruits you encourage are
what people see in me. I don't need to show off to
be a light; I just need to be who I am.

I ask for the gifts of the heart I need to shine.

How did you brighten someone's day today?

Prayer for starting a first job

Spirit of helpfulness, it's time for something
  totally new: a job outside of the house.
Help me to clear my head so that I can pay
  attention to what needs to be done.
Even as the newest or the youngest, there will be
  people relying on me. I can contribute to the
  goals of my new coworkers with every task
  they give me. May I never forget how valuable

each worker is, even once I have
more experience.
With your guidance I can meet the standard set
for me and take pride in my work.
Give me safety and energy on this new adventure,
and when the time comes for my first paycheck,
help me use it wisely and understand even better
the value of hard work.

*Listen carefully to those you meet so that you can
learn to be as helpful as possible.*

Prayer for discerning between good and bad

Spirit who leads, my life is full of choices, some
large, some small. Many things cloud my vision
when I'm trying to choose goodness. I may
be tempted by convenience, or by short-term
pleasure, or by making other people happy. But
choosing what is good is the road to holiness and
integrity. I want to be guided by God's will and to
choose what will lead to justice and love. I want to
choose those things that will help me to be a good
person. You can help me see what is good, and
give me the courage to do it.

At the end of your day, identify the moments when you had a choice to make, and reflect on what motivated your choices.

Prayer to avoid perfectionism

Spirit of goodness, I'm overwhelmed by all that I am supposed to do. What if I make a mistake? My imagination is full of ways that I could flub, and all the problems my errors could cause.

Remind me that the highest standard is love, not flawlessness. I can be loving no matter what else I struggle with, and I can accept love too.

I believe I will be freer when I am not scared of mistakes. You show me that Divine Love is always there for me. Give me freedom, courage, and clearheadedness.

Do something that you have been scared to take on because you worry you won't be good enough.

Generosity

ALL THROUGH THE BIBLE WE FIND GOD GIVING. Jesus's parables illustrate divine generosity, and he gave the greatest gift of all by sacrificing himself on the cross. Generosity is an undeniable value in the reign of God.

Unfortunately, human nature sometimes squelches our generosity. Sometimes we focus on the recipient of our gift, scrutinizing their worthiness. God doesn't do that, though: blessings are given to all, whether or not they "deserve" it. As Dorothy Day wrote, "God help us if we got just what we deserved!" Generosity says more about us as givers than it does about the supposed worthiness of the recipients. Paying attention to others' needs helps us learn how to direct our generosity.

The most frequent call to be generous is to give of our time and attention. Most people, of all ages, backgrounds, and lifestyles, have a fundamental desire to be noticed. It doesn't feel good to have someone look past you or ignore you, so be generous with your attention. It doesn't cost a thing.

Sometimes generosity does cost something, and it's good to start training your heart now not to cling unnecessarily to money. All of us need money to meet our basic needs, but if you're not careful you could start valuing wealth too much and not be able to be as generous as possible. If you start by giving a little when you only have a little, you will feel freer to give a lot if you ever have a lot.

There are many obstacles that discourage us from generosity, such as selfishness, materialism, worry, and distraction. It takes strength to stay generous. The Spirit is there for you as a model and guide, blowing through the world with abundant blessings for all people.

Prayer for a healthy relationship with money

Spirit of abundance, you want all people to have enough. Help me to see what is enough: enough money, enough gadgets, enough things. I don't want to grow into someone who always asks for more than I need, or who lets greed or fear get in the way of being generous.

If I don't have enough, guide me toward the help or opportunity I need.

If I do have enough, guide me to be
that help for others.

You give us so many blessings;
and if a comfortable life is one of them,
I pray to recognize that comfort is just one
of the riches in my life, and to focus my attention
on the things that matter to God.

*If you have the means, find a way to be financially
generous, knowing that if you wait until you feel like
you have "enough," you may never begin.*

Prayer to not be attached to possessions

Spirit who gives us what matters, when I see
through your eyes, I see that my "stuff" only
serves me if it helps me to love better, if it helps
me to be free. There's nothing wrong with finding
pleasure in the things I have. But none of them
will ever love me back, so I shouldn't give too
much of my love or attention to them.

When I cling to things I don't need, remind me
what really matters, so that my possessions don't
possess me.

Give something away, small or large.

Prayer for attentiveness to others

Spirit of selflessness, what can I give? I don't have a lot of money. I haven't found my purpose, the special talent that is only mine to give. But I have another singular gift: my attention.

When I think about the moments that make me feel good, many include having others pay attention to me—not in a showy way, but in a way that lets me know that they see me for who I truly am.

To share that good feeling, I have to slow down and turn my attention outward. I have to value others more than my own rushed schedule. You can give me eyes that see others as you do: with love.

When someone speaks to you, put down whatever you are doing and look at them with your full attention.

Prayer for community service

Spirit of assistance, Jesus came to serve, saying
often that we should do the same. Then he
sent us you, dear Spirit, to remain with us as
we try to be like him.

Service projects are one way to do this—if we are
loving and have a good attitude. Open my eyes
so that I see not just the needs of those I serve,
but their value as well.

Remind me that this experience isn't all about me.
Keep me from self-centeredness.

Help me to learn what I can do quickly and easily
so that I can put my full energy and effort into
serving others.

*The next time you do service, really listen to the
people you are working with, and think about what
you can learn from them.*

Gentleness

GENTLENESS IS NOT ALWAYS ADMIRED IN THIS DAY AND AGE, but it's pretty clear from the Scriptures that God loves gentleness. It's shown in constant mercy, in second, third, and fourth chances, in the compassion of Jesus, and in his ultimate sacrifice.

Gentleness acknowledges all the problems and frustrations of life but acts out of love anyway. Take the father in the story of the prodigal son (Lk 15:11–32). He knows the flaws and sins of his children, but he lets his deep love for them guide his actions.

When you know that love is what you stand for, being gentle doesn't mean you have to be a push-over. You still live according to your standard, but that standard requires a baseline level of care, empathy, and respect even when you are standing up for yourself or dealing with a tough situation.

So how can the Spirit help you grow in gentleness? By reminding you that you are made to love and be loved. By giving you strength to react with thoughtful compassion instead of with fake toughness. By nudging your conscience to resist the gossip, casual cruelty, and negative talk that can come up with friends and classmates. Maybe you'll do more than resist. Maybe you'll set a better, stronger, gentler example.

Gentleness is not weakness, it's a choice to let love be in charge.

Prayer to recognize true strength

Spirit of commitment, you want to help us to grow in gentleness. This is harder to accept than I expected. It frightens me to imagine myself as a pushover, or powerless.

The examples of Jesus and the saints teach me that gentleness has strength in it. You give me the strength to choose to be vulnerable, to choose to listen, to choose to accept others. Making these choices to grow in gentleness takes strength.

Perhaps this is why you come to us with spiritual gifts, because a gentle heart takes strength to cultivate.

When I am tempted to bully or ignore, to close myself off or to overpower others, pour gentleness into my heart and help me to be more like Christ.

When you are faced with a situation in which you could overpower or bully someone, resist the temptation. Later, spend time thinking about how that makes you feel.

Prayer to be a role model

Spirit who leads, I guess I'm old enough now to be a role model. At least, that's what my parents and teachers tell me. I never know who is watching, and I need to think about what other kids might learn from my example. Maybe considering others is the first step in being a role model, because that's what I should show them through my actions: how to care for others more than ourselves.

Give me encouragement and guidance on the way. Help me to see the good impact I have and to be satisfied knowing I did the right thing.

Be attentive to whomever may be looking up to you.

Prayer for when I am sensitive

Spirit of the heart's movement, every feeling I have is stronger than usual. Sometimes my reactions are unusual and surprise the people around me. I don't want people to know how sensitive I am; their jokes and judgment make it worse.

I want to view my emotions as gifts. They are a sign that I am paying attention to life. They help me understand what others are going through. They show my affection and love.

I pray for gratitude, that I can be grateful for every gift you give. I pray that I can work through any emotions that don't feel divinely inspired. I can acknowledge my emotions without letting them control me, because I have both feelings and will. Guide me in balancing these and being patient with myself.

> *Is there something in your life that always brings out a negative emotion? Consider how you can react differently, or if there is a way to avoid that situation, or if there is something you can learn from that reaction.*

Prayer for when I am angry

Spirit of guidance, give me clear vision. Help me to see if my anger is righteous or self-centered. Show me the way to resolve my conflict without hurting anyone.

Sometimes I want to be destructive, even though your way is to build.

Sometimes I want to be harsh, even though your way is gentleness.

Sometimes I let my anger take over, even though your way is to let mercy in.

Soothe any hearts that are on fire with anger, or, if that fire is needed to make the world a better place, help us combine that fire with justice and love.

When you're angry, make sure your reactions leave room for positive outcomes.

Faithfulness

....

BEING FULL OF FAITH: IS IT A FEELING OR A CHOICE?
It may be both. There are times when God's goodness and presence are so obvious that we literally
feel full of emotion. This is a great gift from God!
We can use memories of these moments to inspire
us for years to come. But it's not the only way to
be faithful.

If we rely only on the feeling of faith, we might
not stay faithful for very long. Feelings come and go.
We also make choices about our faith. We return to
prayer even if it feels dry or boring. We remember
Jesus' message to us in the gospel when loving our
neighbor is a challenge. We make worship, service,
and justice into habits, no matter what.

There may be times of doubt. Can you leave
your mind and heart open, just a bit, for God to
sneak into your awareness? The Holy Spirit helps
us with this by inspiring and educating us. Our
response of accepting the Spirit's invitation to faith
can lead us to the feelings—and confirm us in the
choice—of faith.

God's faithfulness to us is eternal, and so is the
invitation to grow in faith.

Prayer for seeking God in the sacraments

Spirit found in all places, sometimes my world
feels very full.

There is so much to see and experience, and it's
easy to seek and find more and more.

I know that I can find you in all places and things,
but I find you especially in the sacraments.

Jesus himself is present and gives himself to me in
the sacrament of the Eucharist.

I know the forgiveness of God in the sacrament
of reconciliation, where I find mercy and love.

And you, generous Spirit, await me in the
sacrament of confirmation, where you will give
me gifts that help me grow in faith.

Remember the experience of one of the sacraments.
Close your eyes and picture the details. As you
envision those things you can remember, thank God
for being present.

Prayer for when I have doubts

Spirit of mystery, the Apostles were in doubt when
you came to them at Pentecost. You came not to
chastise them for their wondering but to inspire
them.

It's possible their confusion and questions never went away, that your presence moved them to remain faithful despite uncertainty. They took Jesus' mission and made it their own.

I trust in your comfort in times of confusion. I don't need to have all the answers, just to let you into the questions and be open to following where you guide.

> *Call to mind something you have never fully understood, or an unanswered question. Work on becoming comfortable with the mystery.*

Prayer for when I need forgiveness

Spirit of renewal, I am ashamed. I have hurt someone. I have not been the best version of myself. I have not followed my values. Now I have to make it right.

Help me see the hurt I have caused and honestly accept my role in it, without excuses. Give me a vision of what repairing that hurt will look like, so that I can overcome my nervousness in asking for forgiveness.

I pray that I will feel you with me when I apologize, and that your peace will help me accept any outcome graciously.

Along with making things right with others, I can also experience mercy and forgiveness in the sacrament of reconciliation. This unconditional love is a great gift, and I am grateful.

Conquer your fear and say you are sorry if you need to.

Prayer to understand the Bible

Spirit who teaches us, the word of God feels distant at times, written long ago in languages and styles that are unfamiliar.

My intellect can help me learn when, why, and how things were written, and to understand the context that shaped the writers whom God inspired.

My heart can be open to how God wants to teach me through the Scriptures now. The word is not limited to long ago but reaches out across time to help me learn and pray.

Each day I can hear your voice in the Scriptures, in a word or phrase or passage. Guide me to look and listen and learn, so that I can know you better.

Choose a line from the Bible and spend a few quiet moments thinking about it.

Modesty

"MODESTY" SHARES THE SAME ROOT (the Latin *modestia*) as words like "moderate" and signifies being "within measure." When we have a sense of our place in the world and don't rely on external affirmation to know who we are, we are able to be modest.

This doesn't just mean knowing our flaws, but knowing our strengths as well, and understanding these are gifts for us to use and develop. They are not markers of our worth.

For most of my teen years I was very insecure, convinced there wasn't much likable about me. I was brash and quirky and needed to grow in self-control. I knew I was talented musically, though, and often hoped people would find out about my musical skill so that they would find me likable. I didn't believe they would like me for any other reason. I had a disordered relationship to both my gifts and my weaknesses. When I grew to accept those as part of the package God built in me, I no longer felt so strong an urge to brag or show off.

Modesty is also used to describe manners of dress, and interpretations of this can vary widely.

Perhaps we could view modesty as a clearheaded-ness about who we are and what we need to share. Immodesty creeps in when we present ourselves in a way that looks for our own worth in the perception of others. We are modest when we present our authentic self, knowing that our worth comes from being children of God.

Prayer to be honest with myself

Spirit of reality, who am I?
What are my strengths?
What are my flaws?
I am still learning.

When I am honest about where I shine, I don't have to show off. When I am honest about where I still need to grow, I learn to be humble. The more I learn that all gifts come from God, the less I crave the attention and approval of others. As I learn who I am, and as I seek praise less, may I learn to share who I am confidently, gifts and flaws, without sharing too much or too little.

If you make a mistake, admit it.

Prayer to keep from bragging

Spirit of self-knowledge, when good things happen, I want people to know! I share my successes with family and friends and enjoy that they are happy for me.

There are times, though, when I cross a line, and sharing good news becomes bragging: when I say something to seem better than others, when my good news hurts someone who might be envious or disappointed, when I'm using my success to try to get others to like me.

I'll try to see the line before I cross it, to be realistic about whom I need to share my triumphs with, and to be equally honest about my struggles.

God doesn't need to hear how great I am to love me, and those who matter most don't either.

Thank you for the signs of love that give me the confidence to hold back sometimes, and to put others' needs before my own.

Talk about someone else's accomplishment.

Prayer to understand others' values

Spirit of perspective, the world doesn't revolve around me.

When someone enjoys something I don't, let me be open to their enthusiasm instead of laughing at it. When someone is fired up about a cause I haven't considered, let me be inspired by their example rather than smirking. When someone is driven to pursue an accomplishment that has never mattered to me, let me be supportive rather than judgmental.

You give each of us different gifts and interests. Help me keep my own in perspective so that I don't make the mistake of thinking the whole world should be like me.

Compliment someone today for something that is unfamiliar to you.

Prayer for use of social media

Spirit of truth, I was created as a child of God. I exist because you loved me into being. I am more than the image I present. I am more than what others perceive. When I change myself to attract people, I am betraying myself by lying about who

I am. When I focus on superficial ways of getting attention, I am betraying myself by denying that I am immensely lovable just as I am.

I pray that I remember this every time I post a photo or a comment, and that I make choices based on who I truly am, and the kind of person I most deeply want to be.

I pray that I learn to be my realest self, not just to act like who I think others want me to be.

I pray that I become even more aware that life is not a performance, but an experience rooted in your uniting love.

> *Each time that you catch yourself worrying about how others perceive you, try to switch your train of thought.*

Self-control

CHANCES ARE YOU HAVE GOTTEN A LOT OF MESSAGES ABOUT SELF-CONTROL: parents, teachers, coaches, babysitters, and older siblings may have all talked to you about this at some point. So maybe you associated it with not calling out in class, or not being a ball hog, or not throwing a tantrum. What if we thought of self-control not as a set of restrictions but as a positive attribute? My favorite translation of the Greek word for self-control is "inner power."

Not only does this remind us what it takes to exercise self-control, it also adds a little clarity about why we do it. Ultimately, you will need to have self-control not because your parents say so but because you want your actions to line up with your values.

I am an impulsive person, and there are many times my impulses don't line up with my values. I may be tempted to make a snide remark, or to talk too much about myself, or to not give enough of myself to others because I am being self-centered. Resisting these temptations requires an inner power, and I never regret letting the Spirit guide me toward self-control.

Another important note: everyone is different, and the area in which you need to grow the most might not be the same as mine. Part of growing up is learning what you need help with. Once you know what that is, just ask for help in prayer. God is always ready to help us grow.

Prayer to manage my emotions

Spirit who holds things together, you can help me understand my emotions: which should inspire me to action, and which I need to consider before I act on them. When I'm angered by injustice, it is good that I am moved to help solve the problem. But when I'm angered by a friend (or by myself), acting impulsively can cause more anger and pain.

I need both strength and wisdom to know what to do with these feelings. Help me use emotion to make the world a better place and to keep my relationships and my heart healthy.

When you feel yourself getting swept up in an emotion, try to name what it is.

Prayer for avoiding gossip

Spirit who loves all people, the temptation to talk about others is strong. I want my friends to think I'm interesting and informed. I want to show I'm in control. But when I give in to temptation and speak critically of others, I'm not in control of my speech. Help me to use words in a way that shows I believe that God loves us and created us with dignity. And when I hear others putting someone down, show me a solution.

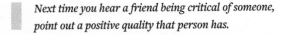

Next time you hear a friend being critical of someone, point out a positive quality that person has.

Prayer for when a friend needs you to listen

Spirit who watches over all, a friend is in trouble and I don't know what to do. Our time together is often lighthearted and fun, but now we might need to be serious.

The best thing I can do is to listen like you would: patiently, attentively, selflessly.

Help me to give my friend the gift of time and attention, resisting the urge to jump into solving the problem, or to make it all about me. By listening, I may learn if there is more my friend needs from me. But I can't discover that without patient listening, without thinking more about others than about myself.

> *Reflect on your conversations with others recently. Was there anything you missed because you were too focused on yourself?*

Prayer for self-discipline

Spirit of constant learning, there is a battle in my will between what I want in the moment and what will give the best long-term result. Which is really me? The impulsive side moved by emotions and appetites, or the part of me that is more thoughtful and considerate?

When I choose homework over games, family time over my phone, punctuality over tardiness, reflective silence over reflexive speech, I grow in self-discipline. You can teach me to do this by showing me why those are choices that help me grow in virtue, and by showing me that I don't deny myself by being self-disciplined. Rather, I grow into a newer version of myself.

> *Think before you act.*

Chastity

THE HUMAN HEART IS MADE FOR RELATIONSHIPS. God made us for love.

Maybe this is obvious, but relationships of all kinds can be tricky. They involve other people, who can surprise or perplex us. They involve emotions, which can also be perplexing! They are the most important thing in our lives because they involve exploring the mystery of another person, but we have to accept that no matter how close we are to our family and friends, they will always be a mystery to us.

Chastity is about relationships and how we express ourselves in those relationships. Living chastely means always examining your relationships in light of your age, state in life, and other commitments.

What makes a relationship appropriate? First, if it fits with the rest of your reality. As a married person, the only romantic relationship that fits in my life is with my husband. As a young person living with your parents or guardians, an intense, time-consuming relationship wouldn't fit for you. As someone who is still learning what kind of life you want to have, a relationship involving permanent commitment doesn't fit.

Most relationships involve expressions of affection, including physical expressions. You might hug your friends when you see them, kiss your parents goodnight, or pat a teammate on the back. As we grow into romantic relationships, we also grow in expressions of affection. Your level of physical expression should match your level of emotional involvement, which comes with time, maturity, and formal commitment. Sexual activity belongs in a fully committed and mature relationship, with commitment having been fully expressed in marriage vows.

Where you should be on the spectrum of physical affection is part of living this virtue of chastity. There will be plenty of roadblocks to confuse you. Entertainment rarely gives us models of resisting the impulses that make us want to be intimate in ways our hearts aren't ready for. The Spirit's gift of chastity can help you know what's right, what fits, and what makes you happy and healthy—body, mind, and soul. Cooperating with the Spirit takes self-control and self-knowledge.

Chastity is often presented as someone's list of dos and don'ts, but when we listen to the deepest desires of our hearts and consider how we want to treat others and be treated, chastity grows in our own hearts.

Prayer for falling in love

Spirit of intensity, help me to love well.
I will fall in love many times in my life: with
    projects, with places, with ideas, with friends,
    with crushes, maybe someday with a spouse
    and with my children.
Every love is a little bit different.
Passion is a gift from God; God wants me to love.
Part of growing up is learning to love properly,
    and understanding the many types of love
    in my life.
Guide me toward loving things
    that help me to grow.
Guide me toward loving people
    who help me be myself.
Guide me toward loving experiences
    that make me even more loving.

When you imagine falling in love, imagine how it fits in with all the other kinds of love in your life.

Prayer for when I have a crush

Spirit of excitement, I am entirely, ferociously, drawn to a new person. This excitement feels like it controls my life. Thoughts of them are out of proportion to the rest of my thoughts. All I want is to be near this person.

I don't really want you to make these feelings go away, but maybe your guidance could help me put them in the proper place. You can help me see how many people in my life love me.

Help me say hi to them without it feeling like that's the most important thing in the world. Let my desire to connect be healthy. If we do connect help me to see this as one of the many connections in my life and to grow into the relationship that is best for us at this time in our lives.

Pray for your crush today. What do you really want for them?

Prayer to understand my body

Spirit of breath, what does it mean to have a body?

Saints and thinkers have written about that for years. That doesn't help me much when I seem to wake up different every day. My body is how I exist in the world and how I interact with others. What I do with it matters.

It will always be changing in age and size, and may also change in disability or illness. It feels hunger and thirst, fatigue and excitement. Help me to learn to listen to what it is telling me, and to learn whether those messages are from God or from the darkness.

As I breathe you in and out, I pray that my comfort grows, that I learn to keep my body healthy, and to cherish it as a great gift.

> *If paying too much attention to your appearance is a temptation for you, avoid spending time in front of the mirror. Think about how God sees you instead.*

Prayer to know my deepest desires

Spirit of purity, help me to understand what I truly, deeply want. My own purity comes not from rejecting every want but from pursuing only my purest desires: those that lead me to a deep, pure love.

I'm entering a time of life when it's easy to confuse the pull of my hormones with the call to a deeper desire, but when I pause and access the hidden corners of my soul, what I find there is a longing for goodness and fidelity, for relationships that last, for a life that inspires.

Bless me with moments that reveal these truest longings, and with the wisdom and will to pursue them above all else.

When you find yourself wanting something, pause and examine if it is a sign that you are really seeking something deeper.